Pebble® Plus

SPORTS STARS

STARS OF PRO WRESTLING

by Mandy R. Marx

Consulting Editor: Gail Saunders-Smith, PhD

CAPSTONE PRESS
a capstone imprint

Pebble Plus is published by Capstone Press,
1710 Roe Crest Drive, North Mankato, Minnesota 56003
www.capstonepub.com

Library of Congress Cataloging-in-Publication Data
Cataloging-in-Publication Data is on file with the Library of Congress.
ISBN 978-1-4914-0594-9 (library binding)
ISBN 978-1-4914-0628-1 (ebook PDF)

Editorial Credits
Erika L. Shores, editor; Juliette Peters, designer; Eric Gohl, media researcher; Tori Abraham, production specialist

Photo Credits
BigStockPhoto.com: EricBVD, 1; Corbis: ZUMA Press/Leonard Ortiz, 9; Newscom: MCT/Red Huber, 7, ZUMA Press/Breaker, 21, ZUMA Press/Leonard Ortiz, 5, ZUMA Press/Matt Roberts, cover, 11, 13, 15, 19, WENN Photos, 17

The author dedicates this book to all of the amazing wrestlers
and wrestling coaches in her life.

Note to Parents and Teachers

The Sports Stars set supports national social studies standards related to people, places, and culture. This book describes and illustrates stars of professional wrestling. The images support early readers in understanding the text. The repetition of words and phrases helps early readers learn new words. This book also introduces early readers to subject-specific vocabulary words, which are defined in the Glossary section. Early readers may need assistance to read some words and to use the Table of Contents, Glossary, Read More, Internet Sites, and Index sections of the book.

Printed in China.
032014   008085LEOF14

Table of Contents

Get in the Ring!

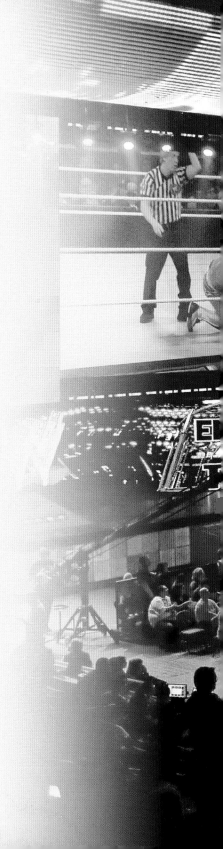

Pro wrestlers have loud mouths,

big bodies, and bad attitudes!

Fans fill arenas to watch

them rumble.

4

Randy Orton

At age 24 Randy Orton became the youngest WWE World Heavyweight Champion. Randy is from a famous family of wrestlers.

WWE stands for World Wrestling Entertainment.

CM Punk

CM Punk won the Money in
the Bank match two years
in a row. Winning this match
lets a wrestler take on anyone
at any time for the championship.

Rey Mysterio

Rey Mysterio is small but tough.

He wrestled Kurt Angle and

Randy Orton at the same time.

He beat them to win the WWE

World Heavyweight Championship.

S.A.F.E
SECURIT

Triple H

For 20 years Triple H has
faced the WWE's top wrestlers.
He has won the WWE World
Championship 13 times.

Undertaker

Undertaker is the king

of WrestleMania.

In 20 years he has never

lost this yearly event.

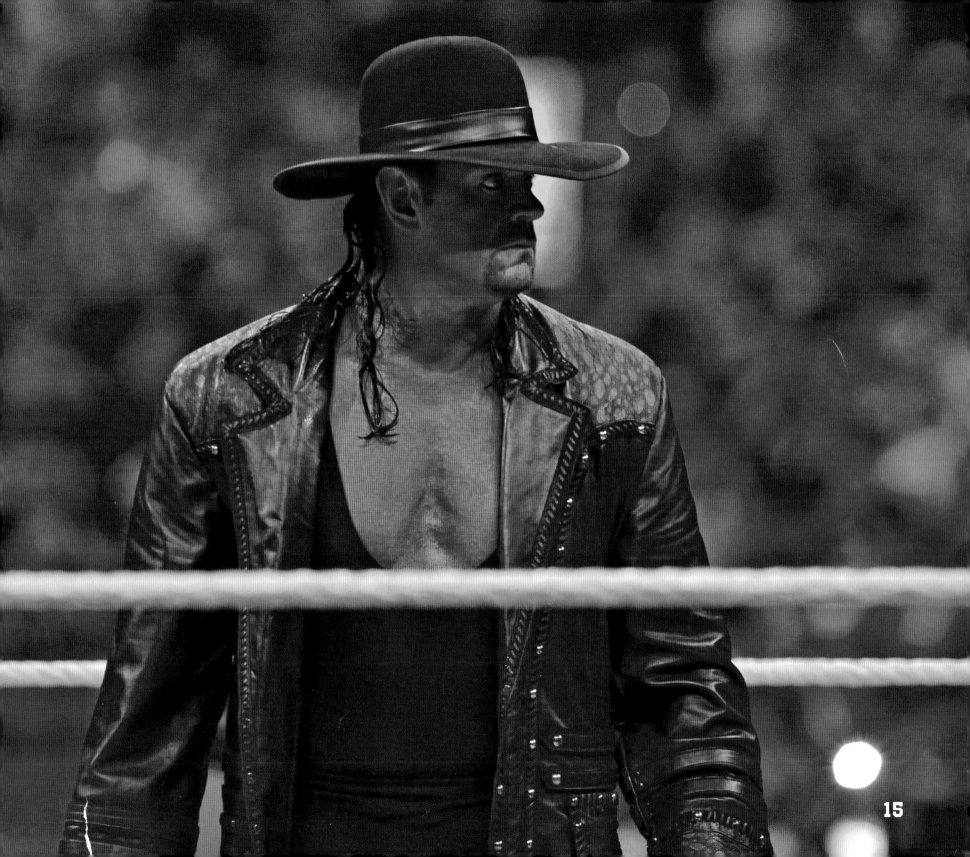

Sheamus

Sheamus is the first
Irish-born wrestler to win
a WWE Championship.
He beat John Cena for the title.

Chris Jericho

Chris Jericho has won the Intercontinental Championship nine times. That's more than any other wrestler.

John Cena

Superstar John Cena started wrestling in the WWE in 2002. He has won 11 WWE Championships and two World Heavyweight titles.

Glossary

arena—a large building in which sports events are held

attitude—the way a person feels

championship—a contest or final match of a series that decides which athlete or team is the overall winner

famous—to be known about by many people

Money in the Bank—a prize that a wrestler can use to challenge a title holder at any time

title—an award given to the champion of a sport

WWE—World Wrestling Entertainment

Read More

Brickweg, Jason. *Chris Jericho.* Pro Wrestling Champions. Minneapolis: Bellwether Media Inc., 2013.

Kaelberer, Angie Peterson. *Cool Pro Wrestling Facts.* Cool Sports Facts. Mankato, Minn.: Capstone Press, 2011.

Stone, Adam. *The Undertaker.* Pro Wrestling Champions. Minneapolis: Bellwether Media Inc., 2012.

Internet Sites

FactHound offers a safe, fun way to find Internet sites related to this book. All of the sites on FactHound have been researched by our staff.

Here's all you do:

Visit *www.facthound.com*

Type in this code: 9781491405949

Index

Word Count: 183
Grade: 1
Early-Intervention Level: 18